Backyard Bird Watchers

A Bird Watcher's Guide to
ROBINS

By

Rebecca Carey Rohan

Gareth Stevens
PUBLISHING

Please visit our website, www.garethstevens.com. For a free color catalog of all our high-quality books, call toll free 1-800-542-2595 or fax 1-877-542-2596.

Cataloging-in-Publication Data

Rohan, Rebecca Carey.
A bird watcher's guide to robins / by Rebecca Carey Rohan.
p. cm. — (Backyard bird watchers)
Includes index.
ISBN 978-1-4824-3907-6 (pbk.)
ISBN 978-1-4824-3908-3 (6-pack)
ISBN 978-1-4824-3909-0 (library binding)
1. American robin — Juvenile literature. 2. Bird watching — Juvenile literature. I. Rohan, Rebecca Carey, 1967-. II. Title.
QL696.P288 R64 2016
598.8'42—d23

First Edition

Published in 2016 by
Gareth Stevens Publishing
111 East 14th Street, Suite 349
New York, NY 10003

Copyright © 2016 Gareth Stevens Publishing

Designer: Laura Bowen
Editor: Therese Shea

Photo credits: Cover, p. 1 (robin) Danita Delimont/Gallo Images/Getty Images; cover, pp. 1–32 (paper texture) javarman/Shutterstock.com; cover, pp. 1–32 (footprints) pio3/Shutterstock.com; pp. 4–29 (note paper) totallyPic.com/ Shutterstock.com; pp. 4–29 (photo frame, tape) mtkang/Shutterstock.com; p. 5 PernilleTofte/Folio Images/Getty Images; p. 7 Brian Guest/Shutterstock.com; p. 9 (European robin) Menno Schaefer/Shutterstock.com; p. 9 (American robin) Sarah Jessup/Shutterstock.com; p. 11 Cindy underwood/Shutterstock.com; p. 13 D and D Photo Sudbury/ Shutterstock.com; p. 15 Jordan Feeg/Shutterstock.com; p. 17 Hway Kiong Lim/Shutterstock.com; p. 19 Steven Grogger/ Shutterstock.com; p. 20 Cheryl E. Davis/Shutterstock.com; p. 21 Martha Marks/Shutterstock.com; p. 22 Chris Hill/ Shutterstock.com; p. 23 Art Wittingen/Shutterstock.com; p. 25 Beth Whitcomb/Shutterstock.com; p. 27 operative401/ Shutterstock.com; p. 29 Tony Campbell/Shutterstock.com.

Printed in the United States of America

CPSIA compliance information: Batch #CW16GS: For further information contact Gareth Stevens, New York, New York at 1-800-542-2595.

CONTENTS

Words in the glossary appear in **bold** type the first time they are used in the text.

A NEW HOBBY

The Real Early Birds

The saying "the early bird gets the worm" may be about robins! They're some of the first birds to chirp in the morning, and they like to eat worms.

I've decided to start a new hobby: bird-watching. When I woke up this morning, I could hear birds in my backyard. They sounded like they were saying, "Yoo hoo! Yoo hoo!" and "Cheer-up, cheerily! Cheer-up, cheerily!"

I looked out the window and saw the singing birds. My mom said they're called robins, and they're one of the first birds we can hear singing in the spring. So, they're the first birds I'm going to write about in my new bird-watching **journal**!

My journal will help me keep track of all the birds I see and what they do.

READY TO OBSERVE

My Bird-Watching Tools

- ☑ binoculars
- ☑ journal
- ☑ pen or pencil
- ☑ camera
- ☑ books about robins
- ☑ computer

My grandpa gave me some things to help me with my bird-watching. He got me a pair of **binoculars**. When I use the binoculars, I can see the robins really well! Grandpa's going to let me use his camera to take pictures, too.

Even though people sometimes call them "robin redbreasts," robins' chest feathers aren't really red. They're more orange. Robins also have a yellow beak and white and black feathers on their throat. There's a white ring around each of their eyes.

Robins have many **distinct** marks. Male robins have a darker head than females.

7

POPULAR BIRDS

Robins' Range

The colored area on this map shows where robins can be found year round. In summer, they may be north of this area. In winter, they may be south.

North America

Robins are very popular in the United States. They're the state bird of Connecticut, Michigan, *and* Wisconsin. The robins we see in the United States and Canada are called American robins. They were named after a bird in Europe.

European robins look different than our robins. European robins are smaller and rounder, with an orange-red face and chest. The rest of their feathers are white and gray. European robins are the national bird of the United Kingdom.

European robin

Field marks are the special stripes, spots, **patterns**, and colors on a bird's body. The field marks of the American robin and the European robin are different.

American robin

9

MAKING A HOME

Nesting Shelf

I made a nesting shelf for robins with my mom. We followed these steps:

1. Nail three boards together to make a floor, wall, and roof. No sides or front are needed.

2. Attach the shelf to the shady side of a building near a muddy place, such as a garden.

3. Wait for robins to build a nest there!

Today, I saw two robins flying in and out of the yard. It looks like they're building a nest!

Robins like to build nests in bushes and trees, where they'll be hidden by leaves and branches. They make their nests out of grass, twigs, feathers, paper, string, and other matter.

They mix it all with mud. They use their beak and wings to make the nest into a cup shape. They line the nest with fresh grass to help make a soft place for their eggs.

Female robins do most of the work to make the cup-shaped nest.

11

EGGS!

Colored by Nature

The color of robin eggs is so pretty that people copy it to make crayons, markers, and paint.

Robins built a nest on my nesting shelf! There are four eggs in the nest. They're a blue color. Some people call this color "robin's-egg blue"! A group of eggs is called a clutch. Most robins have two clutches every spring. Each clutch usually has three to seven eggs in it.

The mother robin sits on her clutch to keep it warm while the baby birds grow in their eggs. This is called **incubation**. It takes 12 to 14 days for robin eggs to **hatch**.

It's easy to spot robin eggs because of their pretty blue color.

13

EATING OUT

A Robin's Menu

- berries
- bugs
- caterpillars
- fruit
- grasshoppers
- snails
- spiders
- worms

Robins like to eat bugs, spiders, caterpillars, and many other creepy-crawly creatures. They like fruit, especially berries, too.

The male robin has been busy looking for food for the female while she incubates the clutch. He spends a lot of time hopping around on the lawn. There, he can find lots of worms—their favorite food!

Robins **tilt** their head to one side when they're trying to find worms. They do this because of the way their eyes work.

Robins find tasty treats like this in the soft ground!

15

A ROBIN'S-EYE VIEW

NEW WORD!

<u>monocular</u>: about or affecting only one eye

Robins have monocular eyesight, which means each eye is used separately.

People once thought robins tilted their head so they could hear worms moving in the soil. Later, scientists found out robins did this because of their special eyesight.

Robins have one eye on each side of their head. They can see to the side and to the front at the same time. However, they can only **focus** through the center of each eye. That's why they tilt their head to one side when they're looking for a nice, fat worm!

This robin has to turn its head to get a good look at something.

17

FEEDING THE FAMILY

When the eggs hatch, the mother and father will be very busy feeding their babies. Robin parents might bring 100 meals a day to the nest! I thought about building a bird feeder to help them, but I remembered that robins don't really like seeds.

My mom and I decided to put some small berries, raisins, and apple pieces on the ground. We'll also buy some mealworms at the pet store and put them out when the time comes.

Robins may try to carry as much food as they can fit in their beak.

19

WELCOME TO THE WORLD

The baby robins have hatched! They're cheeping loudly in the nest because they're hungry. It seems like they're never full! They need a lot of food to grow strong enough to leave the nest.

The mother robin sits on her **brood**. This helps keep them warm until they grow real feathers. Baby robins have some tiny feathers called **down** on their body, but not much. They stay in the nest while they grow more feathers.

This mother robin is sitting on her babies to keep them warm.

21

ROBINS' ENEMIES

This morning, I saw the father robin hopping around the backyard and flicking his tail. He was chirping loudly. Then, I saw the neighbor's cat in the yard. The robin's chirp was an alarm call. Either the mother or father bird will make an alarm call if they feel they or their babies are in danger.

Robins have many predators, including cats, hawks, and large snakes. Squirrels, chipmunks, raccoons, crows, and jays try to eat robin eggs and **nestlings**.

Crows look for
robin eggs and
nestlings to eat.

23

GROWING UP

Baby Robin Numbers

- usually 3 to 7 eggs in 1 clutch
- hatch after 12 to 14 days of incubation
- leave nest 14 to 16 days after hatching
- fly about 2 weeks after leaving nest

The baby birds are about 2 weeks old. They're starting to leave the nest. They can't fly yet, though. So, they follow their father and ask for food. They're learning to find food and water. They stay on the ground, below the nest.

I don't see the mother anymore. She must be getting ready for her second brood. The father will stay with the young for about another 2 weeks. That's when they'll be able to fly and care for themselves.

This young robin can't fly yet. My dad told me to stay away from it while the father robin helps it eat. I might scare the father away.

EMPTY NEST

Helpful Robins

- spread seeds from berries they eat, helping plant growth

- eat bugs that are pests

All the baby robins are gone. The nest is empty. I'm going to leave it where it is, though. Robins return to the same nesting area every year. They might reuse a nest if it's in good shape.

I'm going to keep watch to find out if the robins in my yard fly south in the fall. Some robins remain year round, and some **migrate** short distances in the spring and fall. It depends if they can find enough food where they live.

MAKING FEATHERED FRIENDS

Keep a Field Journal

When I see new birds, I'll make notes of these things to help me figure out what kind of birds they are:

- Date
- Where I Saw It
- How Many?
- Field Marks
- Actions

In winter, robins form flocks, sometimes in the hundreds! They spend the colder months in forests where it's easy to find berries. Sometimes they're only a few miles from where they spent spring and summer. That's why robins are seen so early in the spring—they don't have to travel far!

I've learned so much about robins in just a few weeks. Next, I'm going to learn about other birds I've seen in my backyard. I love bird-watching!

In the colder months, robins can't find worms or bugs in the hard ground. So, they eat a lot of berries.

GLOSSARY

binoculars: handheld lenses that make objects seem closer

brood: a group of young birds that were all born at the same time

distinct: clearly different

down: the soft, fluffy first feathers of a young bird

focus: to see something clearly

hatch: to break out of an egg

incubation: the act of sitting on eggs so they will be warm and will hatch

journal: a book in which one writes down what happens to them or their thoughts

migrate: to move from one area to another for feeding or having babies

nestling: a young bird that has not left the nest

pattern: the way colors or shapes happen over and over again

tilt: to set something at an angle rather than straight up or down

FOR MORE INFORMATION

Books

Amstutz, L. J. *Robins*. North Mankato, MN: Capstone Publishers, 2016.

Mara, Wil. *Robins*. New York, NY: Cavendish Square, 2015.

Wolf, Sallie. *The Robin Makes a Laughing Sound: A Birder's Journal*. Watertown, MA: Charlesbridge, 2010.

Websites

American Robin
www.all-birds.com/American-Robin.htm
See photos and videos of robins, and listen to their songs.

American Robin
www.biokids.umich.edu/critters/Turdus_migratorius
Many questions about robins are answered here.

INDEX